To Marino

Live your best life!

Teresa
de Grosbois

Text copyright © 2008 by Small Shifts Books & Media Inc
Illustrations copyright © 2008 by Jennifer Llewellyn-Pollack
All rights reserved.

Second Printing, 2008

Small Shifts Books & Media Inc,
Website: www.smallshifts.com
info@smallshifts.com

Canadian Cataloguing in Publication Data
de Grosbois, Teresa M., 1964 –
   The Presents' Presents

ISBN: 978-0-9809484-2-4 (bound) – ISBN 978-0-9809484-0-0 (pbk)

I. Llewellyn-Pollack, Jennifer 1982 II. Title

Printed and Bound in China.

The Presents' Presents!
Written by: Teresa de Grosbois
Ilustrated by: Jennifer Llewellyn-Pollack

For my Daughter Rae on her eleventh birthday
with grateful thanks to the other children who inspired this story:
Fiona, Holly, Maggie, Jennifer, Julia, and Josie

This book belongs to:

_____

When Rae was only five
She got a special bear.
It had a heart inside
And a little suit to wear.

Each time she got some money,
The thing Rae always chose
Was to buy her special bear
A brand new set of clothes.

"Are you buying presents for your present?"
Mom asked with some surprise!
"Yes" she told Mom sweetly.
"Dear, do you think that's wise?"

"My bear will need a toy soon!"
Rae said with earnest care.
"She'll be lonely otherwise:
She needs a baby bear!"

So when Rae turned six
She got a baby bear.
It needed new clothes too,
Even socks and underwear.

So they bought presents for the present,
Then the present's present too,
'Til soon Rae's room was full:
You barely could walk through!

The seventh birthday present?
It was a fashion doll.
It got more clothes than Rae did,
And a house to keep it all!

Then when Rae turned eight
She got an electronic pet.
She fed and changed and loved it
And kept it from all threat.

Mom noticed that she played with it
For hours each evening.
Rae told her "Mom, I need some points,
To buy it a new thing!"

"Oh dear!" said Mom with worry.
"I do not like this trend.
Presents needing presents!
When will this thinking end?"

And for her ninth birthday
Rae got a small stuffed toy;
With an internet account.
Oh what blissful joy!

And Rae would play for hours
To buy its virtual home,
With many rooms and play things
Where her small Web friend could roam.

And the special bear's large family
Continued needing clothes.
And the electronic pet?
She now had **three** of those!

And so this trend continued
As Rae grew big and smart.
While Mom and Dad kept wondering
"Where did this thinking start?"

So they bought presents for the presents
And the present's presents too,
Until those poor tired parents
Had their faces turning blue!

Then one day Rae's young sister
Asked to "present present" shop;
When Mother nearly lost it
And told Fiona "STOP!"

"NO MORE PRESENTS FOR THE PRESENTS!"
Mom firmly stood her ground,
"It's time I put my foot down
And turned this trend around!"

And so for Rae's tenth birthday
She considered Mom's new stand:
How the presents for the presents
Were getting out of hand.

Rae talked to her friend Josie:
They agreed they'd had enough.
"Do we really need so much
Of all this same old stuff?"

They decided one big party
Was best for them that year;
But what to do for presents
With the party drawing near?

"Could we pick a needy cause?" Dad said,
"And ask each child to bring
Perhaps a gift of money
To do some worthy thing?"

So Rae and Josie pondered
And decided what to do.
They helped to buy a bigger home
For a Lemur at the Zoo!

Then Fiona asked if her next gift
Could be a foster child.
"I'll give up all my treats," she said.
"OK," Mom said and smiled.

And a Guatemalan girl
Was given sponsor care
That gave her school a bit each month
And clothes for her to wear.

Soon some of their close friends
Got caught up in the mood.
Maggie's birthday fed a family
Through the local bank of food.

The next year Josie helped
A giraffe at the local Zoo.
And a Tanzanian school
Got help from Holly too.

Jennifer used her birthday gifts
To help scientists ensure
When women get breast cancer
Their doctors find their cure.

And money raised
On Julia's day
Gave homeless pets
A place to stay.

So each on her birthday
Picked some special need
And friends brought gifts of money
To help with some good deed.

As Rae turned eleven
She asked, "Now what this year?"
"Some children need your help"
Mom said, "would you like to hear?"

Mom described a charity
Started by her friend,
To help children in Africa
Who needed help to fend.

"Its name is *Inspire Africa.*
They'll build a clinic and a school
And a hall where children meet.
You know what's really cool?

These children **want** to go to school!
It means a better life.
With schooling they can get a job
To buy food and end their strife.

And it gets dark there early;
Their houses have no light,
They'll build a hall that's lit:
A place to read at night."

When Rae turned eleven
The truly great surprise
Was children of Rwanda
Were given better lives.

They all bought presents with their presents
For others with some need.
Who knows what future leaders
May grow from each small deed!

A Note to Parents and Teachers

This book helps children to understand the impact of their choices on themselves and on others. It offers a simple philosophy for children: to understand the difference between happiness which comes from the possession of "things" and happiness which comes from looking inside ourselves to find our connection with others. The "having" of things is quickly replaced by the "wanting" of more things. It does not bring a lasting happiness. A choice to focus more on our relationship to others and to ourselves brings a more lasting happiness.

If you are interested in exploring these concepts more from an adult perspective, I recommend the books of Deepak Choprah, Ekhart Tolle and Brandon Bays.

"... happiness for a reason is just another form of misery because the reason can be taken away from us at any time."

Deepak Choprah, Power Freedom and Grace

Hey Kids!

Be a Birthday Super Hero

Visit
www.smallshifts.com for ideas!
Click on
Superheroes!

Email us at Heroes@smallshifts.com and tell us what you supported.
We'll send you a free online activity or coloring book.
"You can make the difference!"